Arthur O'Leary

A Review of the Important Controversy

Between Dr. Carroll and the Rev. Messrs. Wharton and Hawkins

Arthur O'Leary

A Review of the Important Controversy
Between Dr. Carroll and the Rev. Messrs. Wharton and Hawkins

ISBN/EAN: 9783337102814

Printed in Europe, USA, Canada, Australia, Japan

Cover: Foto ©ninafisch / pixelio.de

More available books at **www.hansebooks.com**

A REVIEW

OF THE

IMPORTANT CONTROVERSY

BETWEEN

Dr. CARROLL and the Reverend Meſſrs. WHARTON and HAWKINS;

INCLUDING A DEFENCE OF THE

Conduct of Pope CLEMENT XIV. (GANGANELLI) in ſuppreſſing a late religious Order:

IN A LETTER TO A GENTLEMAN,

By the Rev. ARTHUR O'LEARY.

To which is annexed,

A LETTER FROM CANDOUR

TO THE

Right Honourable LUKE GARDINER;
On his Bill for the Repeal of a Part of

The Penal Laws

Againſt the IRISH CATHOLICS.

LONDON:
Printed for, and ſold by the Editor, P. KEATING,
No. 4, Air-Street, Piccadilly, MDCCLXXXVI.

BOSTON PUBLIC LIBRARY

Entered at Stationer's Hall.

THE EDITOR to the PUBLIC.

SINCE the most distinguished Characters of the present Day have borne such ample Testimony to the Candour, as well as to the Eminent Abilities of our Author, the very Name of O'LEARY *carries with itself* such weight *and is become so respectable amongst the liberal minded of every description, as to render Panegyric both vague and superfluous. The Productions therefore of his animated Pen, cannot fail to awake the attention of all Parties; more especially when employed on a Subject of so interesting a Nature as the following.*

A REVIEW

OF THE

IMPORTANT CONTROVERSEY

BETWEEN

Doctor CARROLL and the Reverend Meffrs. WHARTON and HAWKINS, including, &c.

SIR,

UNTIL within thefe few days, I have not had time to give the three pamphlets you were fo kind as to fend me from London, a perufal; much lefs have I had leifure to digeft my remarks on them, with that deliberaton, which the importance of the fubject in debate requires. In the firft, (which appears to have given birth to the other two) the Author, who ftyles himfelf *late Chaplain to the Catholics of Worcefter*, complains of two heavy and unwarrantable conftraints, under which he laboured, whilft he profeffed himfelf a catho-

catholic clergyman; the one, a prohibition to chufe his religion from fcripture, *according to his fancy*; the other, which feems to him ftill more grievous, is, the being debared the privilege of taking to himfelf *a female helpmate*, by whofe affiftance he might be enabled to explain them in a more *fenfible* manner. The fecond I perceive is written by another clergyman, who, from fimilar motives with the gentleman juft mentioned, has alfo read his recantation: hitherto this gentleman has not favoured the world with any treatife calculated to reform the vitiated morals of a corrupt age; but for this omiffion he has made ample amends, by contributing to the propagation of the human fpecies, as well by his example, as by his celebrated *treatife againft celibacy*. If virginity be a monfter, *monftrum horrendum ingens*, he is to be ranked in the front of thofe heroes who are ready to encounter and deftroy it. The third has for its author an orthodox divine, Dr. Carroll, who has blended the politenefs of a gentleman, with the erudition of a fcholar, and the information of an able writer: of him I fhall take occafion to make mention at the clofe of my letter.

As

As to the two former, I should have left them for ever in the undisturbed enjoyment of their PRIESTESSES, and the propagation of their *mixed religious race*, had they not revived those controversies, which the liberality of an enlightened and philosophic age has doomed to doze on the shelves of college libraries : or had they not made the ungenerous attempt to draw on the English catholics the hatred of their protestant neighbours, by the revival of the hackneyed charge of their denouncing damnation against heretics, and the prohibition of scriptural information.

HAD not the POSTSCRIPT to the London edition of Dr. Carroll's Address, suggested the real motives of these pretended conversions, the complaints of the converts themselves *against chastity*, and their subsequent conduct, would have enabled me to form my conjectures. One of them sets forth with the modesty of a vestal;* the *Postscript* removes the veil with a *gentle hand*, and exposes a ⸺.

* Mr. W-rt-n in his Letter to the Catholics of Worcester.

As to the remark in the poftfcript, quoted from the celebrated author of the Internal Evidence of the Chriftian Religion, *Soame Jennings, Efq.* in which he fets *the unbridled paffions of man*, at variance with *his judgment*, and afcribes the victory to the former, when he yields to their fway; never was a maxim in ethics better founded in truth, nor more applicable to the cafe of Meffrs. Wh-rt-n and H-k-ns.

The corruption of the heart, leads infenfibly to the errors of the mind. Soloman himfelf, the wifeft of men, gave too great a fcope to his paffion for women, before he offered facrifice to idols. Perhaps he acted in contradiction to his judgment :———the fame might have been the cafe with thefe gentlemen, when they both trampled on their vows of chaftity, the obfervance of which, they would not have found fo difficult, had they continued in the practice of the evangelical precepts, WATCH AND PRAY. They now amufe the public with apologies for their conduct; but the judicious part of the public will ever fufpect the candour of apologies, which originate in fenfuality,

and

and the love of carnal pleasures. Our passions may engage us in faults, which however we may attempt to reconcile to ourselves, by silencing the voice of conscience, still expose us to public censure. Pride steps in as an auxiliary to palliate our crimes; and hence the apologies of our religious changelings to justify the *wanton breach* of the vows they made to God.

WHEN these gentlemen exchanged their breviaries for *Calvides Lætus's Callipedia,** and their sacerdotal vestments for the *cestus of Venus*, the catholics of England did not ring the alarm bell: they considered the separation of such persons as no loss to their religion; nor as *any precious acquisition* to that which they

---

* The Art of begetting pretty Children, an heroic poem, written in elegant Latin verse, in which all the rules of that art are laid down; RULES by far more agreeable to flesh and blood, than the rules of a ST. BENEDICT OR IGNATIUS. How far the study of them may tend to influence the features of Messrs. H-k-ns and Wh-rt-n's children, I will not take upon me to say; of this however I am certain, that all over Europe, the children of those who have taken orders in the Roman church (next to hangmen and priestcatchers) make the most forbidding appearance.

feigned

feigned to embrace: they knew, that a catholic clergyman, who tramples on his vows, renounces his breviary, and deserts the sacred altar, would as soon become a turkish *Iman* at Constantinople as *a parson* in England, were it not through the dread of the operation of the circumcision knife.

In return for the support which they gave these gentlemen whilst they were strangers to their foibles, the catholics of Worcester had aright to expect that their religion would not be bandied about in flying pamphlets, in order again to become the topic of conversation, amongst an inspired rabble, who, with similar religious libels to their chaplain's letter in the one hand, and a faggot in the other, attempted to plunder the Bank, and lay the capital of England in ashes, in the year 1780, under pretence of purging the land from the errors of popery.*

---

* Mr. Westley's Letter in Defence of the Protestant Associations—their Appeal to the People of Great Britain——and several other fanatical publications were industriously circulated about that time, for the laudable purpose of fanning the embers of popular prejudice against popery: the flames of which at last
burst

In the choice of spiritual guides, it is more prudent in the catholics of Worcester to follow those whose sincerity they cannot doubt---who are ready to stand or fall with them in the cause of conscience---who prefer penal laws---legal disqualifications and every oppression which the misguided policy of former reigns has imposed on them, to the rights of citizens and flattering prospects of a fleeting life, sooner than violate the obligations they contracted with the Almighty, at the foot of his sacred altar.———it is more prudent in them, I say, to follow such guides,

---

burst forth in so furious a manner, (not only against the chapels, dwelling-houses, &c. of catholics, but also against the habitations of several respectable protestants) that nothing less was expected than the utter extirpation of the constitution in church and state, as well as popery——thus, when the fire of an enthusiastic zeal is once heated, there can be no bounds prescribed to its rage.

"For zeal's a dreadful termagant,
"That teaches *Saints* to tear and rant;
"Turns *meek and secret sneaking ones*
"To rawheads fierce, and bloody-bones:
"And not content with endless quarrels
"Against the wicked, and their morals,
"The *Gibellines*, for want of *Guelfs*,
"*Divert their rage upon themselves.*"

HUDIBRAS.

than

than to follow thofe whofe fincerity they have every reafon to queftion, whom the love of eafe and pleafure has feduced from the fanctity and feverity of the clerical profeffion, and to whom the words of Erafmus, to fimilar apoftates of his time, may be applied, "yefterday a monk, to-day a hufband, and to-morrow a father."

Their late chaplain may fay to the catholics of Worcefter, come and follow me! A *catholic cannot fet out with that freedom of enquiry—read the fcriptures—judge for yourfelves,* &c. The broachers of the moft abominable errors have founded the fame charge, and given the fame falutary advice. Bernard Ochin, the firft general of the capuchins, perfuaded a wench to follow him out of Italy, after he had embraced the new opinions which then began to fpread. Bayle, in his Critical Dictionary, juftifies him in an ironical manner, by faying, *he delivered the young woman out of Babylon,* as Erafmus juftified Ocolampadius upon a fimilar occafion, by faying, *he married a buxom lafs to mortify the flefh.* Ochinus was as celebrated for his learning and knowledge of the fcriptures, as he was renowned

nowned for his oratory in the pulpit. He retired to Poland, where in juftification of his having more wives than one at a time, he publifhed his treatife in favour of poligamy, as Mr. H-k-ns has publifhed his treatife *againſt celibacy*. He fet out with that *freedom of enquiry* fo much recommended by the late chaplain of the catholics of Worcefter—gave *full ſcope to his reſearches*, which were crowned with ATHEISM in his work entitled the Hiftory of (what he calls) the three impoftors, Mofes, Chrift and Mahomet.

NUMBERLESS are the inftances of the monftrous effects of this *freedom of enquiry* propofed by thofe enlightened apoftles, who after having *began with the ſpirit, finiſhed with the fleſh*. In the beginning they affect the ferious folemnity of a tragic writer, by painting, in fable colours, the miferies that attend our fubjection to authority! the misfortunes of the noble foul fhackled in the fetters of obedience to paftors, LIKE A FAIR ZENOBIA IN THE CHAINS OF A TYRANT! our uncharitablenefs, in excluding from eternal blifs, and configning to perdition, chriftians of every defcription except ourfelves!

felves! Thefe are ferious themes, and of fo affecting a nature as to enable a poet of moderate genius to work up a tolerable religious tragedy, were it now the cuftom as in the 14th century to exhibit fuch pieces on the ftage, if at the difcovery or unravelling of the plot they had not the effects of *Comedy*, in exciting the laughter of the audience when they came to know that all this folemn buftle was about *a wife*.

But let us come to the charges fo often exhibited againft catholics, either for the purpofe of ftigmatizing them with ignorance of the knowledge of the fcriptures, to render them contemptible; or with uncharitablenefs in dooming their diffenting fellow chriftians to perdition, to make them the objects of public deteftation; or with an unwarrantable feverity, in laying cruel reftraints on their clergy, to fhew the defpotifm and tyranny of popery. Such accufations operate more effectually on the paffions, than difference of belief in matters purely fpeculative; which Meffrs. W. and H. only flightly glance at. And here I cannot omit the judicious remark of an ingenuous writer,
" *the*

"*the enemies of a religion never understand it, because they hate it; and they often hate it, because they do not understand it; therefore they adopt the most atrocious calumnies against it.*"* How often, and how far this remark has been verified with regard to the catholics of Great Britain and Ireland, is but too well known to the informed and impartial. But, to return to the charges.

The first book that was put into my hands after my spelling book, was the Psalter of David, and the New Testament. A translation of the Old and New Testaments, by the English colleges of Rheimes and Doway, has been in the hands of the catholic laity of these nations for almost these two hundred years past; for the truth of this, I appeal to Messrs. H. and W. themselves. Away then, *for ever*, with so futile and groundless an accusation! It is not the reading the scriptures, but *a false interpretation of them*, that is prohibited amongst us. We believe, that the sacred depositum of faith is committed to the custody of the catholic church, and that she cannot admit its adulteration by the

---

* Gibbon, Essai sur la Literature.

arbitrary interpretations of individuals. She will not, neither can she permit, even the most sage and learned of her doctors to interpret these words, MY FATHER IS GREATER THAN I, in the sense of Socinus or Crellius, who infer from this passage, that the mystery of the trinity is a vulgar error. Neither will she permit them to interpret, I AND MY FATHER ARE ONE, in the sense of the Antitrinitarians, who infer from this passage, not a co-equal and consubstantial, but a *moral union*, such as subsists between God and a justified man in the state of grace; much less will she suffer the rustics of her communion who can but just read, to give a carnal interpretation to the Song of Solomon, so replete with sensible images, that Voltaire, in his Philosophical Dictionary, ridicules it as an *obscene ballad*; and Whiston, who prophesied the downfal of popery in the year of our Lord 1704, uses every argument to destroy its authenticity; altho' protestant churches admit it into the number of their canonical books. We must leave the fate of the dead to HIM that has passed sentence on them; yet, in all human appearance, it would have been better for these two learned blasphemers to have believed more, and read

read lefs; and after a fincere forrow for their fins, to have expired, faying from the bottom of their hearts, " I believe " in the Holy Ghoft, the holy catho-" lic church."

SHE commands the married people of her communion to get their children baptized, though Barclay in his Apology for the Quakers, denies the neceffity of fuch an initiation. She never will permit her brawny peafants to fit down and interpret the impenetrable myfteries of the Apocalypfe, nor fuffer them to fet up evangelical roftrums on Sundays in the ftreets and highways in order to become preachers of new doctrines fafhioned according to their grofs ideas to a rude and illiterate rabble, in imitation of that tall Gofpeller condemned to work in the fortifications of his Pruffian majefty, who after having perfuaded a fet of his deluded followers from the revelations of St. John that he was the perfon mentioned therein appointed to *break the feven feals*, as a proof of his miffion in one day deflowered feven virgins, who were prefented by their mothers to the nuptials of this new meffiah, or *over-grown lamb*.

SHE

She is aware of the horrid consequences attending an uncontrolled interpretation of the scriptures, as well amongst the learned, as the ignorant of her communion; and therefore, although she permits the reading of them, she prohibits any interpretation which may alter that DIVINE FAITH, which she herself *has not the power to change.*——Such as it has been handed down to her, *pure and unaltered from its first source,* such she will transmit it to succeeding generations, to the end of time. In restraining them under such limitations, she effectually guards them against the monstrous, and contradictory doctrines, which are daily springing up, which have sprung up from the very infancy of christianity, and at different periods will spring up till time shall be no more. Thus, the catholic church, like *a fond and tender mother,* cautions her children against unwholesome, poisonous and deadly food.

With regard to those who have been born without her pale, and to whom the errors of their fathers have been transmitted in so long a succession as to make them hereditary, and consequently

quently for the moſt part involuntary, ſhe is more lenient.

No perſon has a right to control or blame her, for keeping her own children within the bounds of ſubordination and due obedience. It is an authority which the confiſtory of Geneva aſſumes to itſelf, and exerciſes over its ſubjects. It burnt Roſſeau's Emilius, though Roſſeau and Shafteſbury acknowledge, that the catholic church could do it with a better grace. The former, in expoſtulating with his countrymen on their conduct towards him, exhorts them, either to follow him in the walks of the religion of nature, or if they aſſume to themſelves any authority in matters of religion, to ſubmit to the authority of the catholic church, which their fathers had quitted; alleging, that he was as free to diſſent from Geneva, as they were from Rome. " Prove to me," *ſays he,* " that there is any authority on " earth to which I am bound to ſubmit, " and to-morrow I'll become a catholic," *Et demain je me fais catholique.*

If any religious communion be authorized to lay down rules for its members,

to command or prohibit what it thinks may promote or obſtruct their ſpiritual welfare, why ſhould the catholic be diveſted of a ſimilar power? Shafteſbury himſelf, who aſcribes her power to the refinement of policy, as all freethinkers aſcribe the eſtabliſhment of chriſtianity to the ſame cauſe, ſays, *he would find the exerciſe of eccleſiaſtical authority more tolerable under ſuch an hierarchy, than under the ſway of thoſe who are eternally contending with her.* " This, ſays he, is
" that antient hierarchy, which in re-
" ſpect of its foundation, its policy, and
" the conſiſtency of its whole frame and
" conſtitution, cannot but appear, in
" ſome reſpect, *auguſt and venerable*, even
" in ſuch as we do not eſteem weak
" eyes. Theſe are the ſpiritual con-
" querors, who like the firſt Cæſars,
" from ſmall beginnings, eſtabliſhed the
" foundation of an almoſt univerſal mo-
" narchy. No wonder if at this day, the
" immediate view of the hierarchial reſi-
" dence, the court and city of Rome,
" be found to have an extraordinary
" effect on foreigners of other later
" churches. No wonder if the amazed
" ſurveyors are for the future ſo apt,
" either to conceive the horrideſt aver-
" ſion

"sion to priestly government, or, on the
"contrary, to admire it so far as to wish
"a coalescence with this antient mother
"church.

"In reality, the exercise of a power,
"however arbitrary or despotic, seems
"less tolerable under such a spiritual
"sovereignty, so extensive, antient, and
"of such long succession, than under
"the petty tyranny, and mimical poli-
"ties of some new pretenders. The
"former, may even persecute with a
"tolerable grace; the latter, who would
"willingly derive their authority from
"the former, and graft on their suc-
"cessive right, must necessarily make
"a very *aukward figure*. And whilst
"they affect the same authority in go-
"vernment, they raise the highest ri-
"dicule in those who have real discern-
"ment, and distinguish originals from
"copies. *O imitatores servum pecus!*"*

When the famous Whiston, whose enlarged powers raised him above all the writers of the eighteenth century, by endowing him with the gift of prophesy,

* Shaftesbury's Characteristics, vol. iii. p. 3{.

whereby he foretold the downfal of popery, the rebuilding of the temple, the reftoration of the Jews, and the peaceful reign of the Millennium, to happen in the year 1714, afterwards in 1735, and at laft, when at the expiration of thefe two periods he found his oracles were not yet accomplifhed, in the year 1766; when the celebrated Whifton, whofe fkill in philofophy, fcripture, and fathers, is fo well known over all the learned world, and who in his Theory of the Earth, has difplayed fuch extenfive knowledge, that we are tempted to believe a pre-exiftent ftate, in which the Author of Nature had put the compaffionate Whifton's hand to defcribe the figure of the earth, and give it what fhape he thought fit; when this great man became an Arian, and wrote to the archbifhops of Canterbury and York the reafons of his feparation from the church of England, thofe prelates exercifed their paftoral jurifdiction in condemning fuch of his works as attacked their creed; and moreover gave him to underftand, that his private judgment, and arbitrary interpretation of fcripture, was not to ftand in competition with authority.

rity. Catholic prelates could do no more.

If the catholics of Worcester followed their late chaplain's advice and example, in setting out on a *religious ramble* they would find the excursion laborious and difficult, amidst the conflict of parties, and variety of religious sects, all appealing to scriptures, and never agreeing amongst themselves. My advice therefore is, that they remain content with the religion of their ancestors—if they should be asked the reason why they prefer it to any other, they can give the same which induced St. Augustin to become a catholic; though in his time there were as many different religions, as there are now; and as many appeals made to scripture. To ask them why they remain as they are, is the same thing as to ask a traveller, why he follows the high road which has been followed for ages. It is the duty of the man who quits it, or who, by curiously seeking after new paths has lost his way, to look about him, and enquire whether he does not go astray.

After the fatal instances of the repeated errors and deviations of so many learned

learned men, from Simon the magician and cotemporary of the apoſtles, to Arius in the fourth century; and from Arius to Mr. Whiſton in the eighteenth, and the numerous erroneous doctrines condemned by the church, in ſo long a ſucceſſion of ages, a catholic muſt acknowledge, that it is hazardous in the extreme to change his creed; and that who ever takes his own private judgment for his guide, in matters of religion, riſques the verifying St. Bernard's remark, that *a man in becoming his own preceptor, often becomes the ſcholar of a fool.*

IF they read the ſcriptures in ſearch of a new religion, whom are the catholics of Worceſter to believe? Chriſt, who commands them *to liſten to the church*, or their late chaplain, who ſays, *liſten not to her?* Chriſt, who ſays, *the gates of hell ſhall never prevail againſt her*; or the chaplain, who ſays, *they have?* a St. Paul who enforces *obedience* to paſtors, conſtituted to watch over, and render an account of their flocks; or the chaplain who preaches *reſiſtance to their authority?* A St. Paul who diſtinguiſhes truth from error, and who aſſerts, that the church is *the pillar of the firſt*, and that the latter muſt be be guarded againſt, or the chaplain who affirms, that the beſt fence againſt error, is to give full ſcope to the fickle mind, and inſtead of embracing the firm *pillar of truth*, to graſp the *ſhaking reed of fancy!* In a word, man muſt be guided, either by his private judgment, or authority in matters of religion: the errors of the learned, and the wild extravagance of the ignorant, who from time to time became their own oracles, evidently demonſtrate, that the firſt is a deceitful guide. If the mind of man then, naturally fickle and unſettled, ſtands in need of a guide in the road to eternal life, *I ſhall never heſitate to take for my guide the catholic church*, which contains in herſelf the authority of paſt and future ages: nor ſhall I run here and there in queſt of my father's legacy, whilſt I have it in my poſſeſſion.

The catholic church has her commiſſion regiſtered in the archives of chriſtianity; it is hers to interpret the law, it is my duty to obey: thus my faith reſembles the pillar which guided the wayfaring Iſraelites; if it has the *darkneſs* of a cloud, it has the *brightneſs* of fire; if it propoſes myſteries wrapped up up in *awful obscurity*; the motives of credibility, and authority on which I believe them, afford *full light* and sufficient evidence to command my assent.

It must then be acknowledged, that the submission of a catholic to the church, is at least as reasonable as that of any other christian to the rules and institutions of the society to which he belongs; and history informs us that these societies were never satisfied their members should believe scripture alone, but insisted moreover that they should interpret them, in the sense received by the pastors and teachers of each society to which they belonged.

In vain do quakers, presbyterians, anabaptists or methodists, open their bibles to prove the purity and sublimity of their respective doctrines; the established church will insist on their finding out the thirty-nine articles in scripture, otherwise she excludes them from her priviliges and benefices. On the other hand, the thirty-nine articles would meet with an unhospitable reception, *as scriptural intruders*, in the kirk of Scotland. Let ecclesiastical authority be ever

ever fo much exploded, as an unfupportable tyranny, 'tis plain that every chriftian fociety exercifes it; and let the right of private judgment be painted as the offspring of Heaven; on earth, individuals muft affimilate its features, to the judgment of the focieties to which they belong.

AFTER the fynod of Dort had terminated the great controverfy in Holland between Gomar and Arminius, concerning predeftination, it was in vain to allege the fcriptures with the right of private judgment. The grand penfionary Barneveldt, fpread his filver locks on the fcaffold at the age of feventy-fix, becaufe he could not believe, that God from all eternity predeftinated mortals to everlafting damnation, without any regard to their bad actions, but merely from his pure will and pleafure. In vain did that venerable fage plead the right of *private judgment*, as the leading principle of the reformation: or that St. Paul declares *that God wills all men to be faved, and come to the knowledge of the truth*; or that God himfelf declares, *he willeth not the death of a finner*. His interpretation of thefe texts, was different from

from that of the synod; and therefore, the executioners axe put an end to the controversy. Grotius, the oracle of kings, would have shared the same fate had he not made his escape from prison, and leaving a rigorous predestination to the Dutch, retired to France to enjoy that freedom, which had been refused him in his own country.

Thus, this liberty, so much extolled in theory, is fettered in practice. And thus, these very societies, who heretofore were its warmest penegyrists at their separation from the catholic church, either punish or disqualify the individuals that belong to them, for reducing to practice what they themselves have recommended, or force them to follow the maxim of the old philosopher, who said, *a wise man should have two religions, one for himself, and another for his country*. In a word, this freedom of interpretation is one of those ideas, which logicians call PHANTASTICAL because they have no conformity with any real architype. In the beginning of these convulsions, tending to overthrow long standing establishments, individuals may take it for their standard; but when they

they form congregations apart, and adopt a settled form of ecclesiastical government, under pastors, superiors, elders, or bishops, call them what you please, they limit and point out the mode of interpretation, and fix *their own* as the standard of orthodoxy.

IF the council of Trent would not permit Luther to interpret scripture in his own way, Luther in his turn, when he became the head of a new religion, with peculiar liturgies, prayer books, and catechisms would not allow Zuinglius, whom he excommunicated, as well as the pope, for not believing his consubstantiation or real presence; Luther, I say, would not suffer the sacramentarians to interpret the gospel as they thought fit. And when Calvin became the MUFTI of Geneva, in opposition to the Roman pontiff, Servetus and others had no alternative to chuse, but the faggot, or Calvin's interpretation of the Bible. How disingenuous therefore are those men, who, to encrease the popular prejudices against catholics, set the profile of the picture to view, and charge to one society, what can evidently be laid to the charge of all; if preventing individuals from becoming, what thefe focieties efteem blafphemers or vifionaries, by a perverfe interpretation of the fcriptures, can be accounted a reproach.

IF thefe refpective focieties affume an abfolute control over their own members, and do not allow them a latitude of interpretation, contrary to the fenfe of the collective body, in the name of heaven has the catholic church lefs authority? or muft her children renounce the apoftle's creed, and the authority of ages, to commence *freethinkers?* Spinoza began, by examining all religions; and finifhed his *free enquiries* by having none: being fo fuccefsful as to difcover there was NO OTHER GOD but the extenfive mafs of nature.

THE catholic therefore is unjuftly upbraided with *flavifh principles.* If he fubmits to authority, he is not in a worfe condition than any other chriftian, who fubmits to the authority of that collective body of which he is a member. The authority to which he fubmits, is the greateft on earth. If he takes fcripture for his guide, he is as well authorized to
inter-

interpret it in a catholic fenfe, as his adverfaries are authorifed, to interpret it in theirs.

But a charge of a more enormous nature is brought againft catholics, by the late chaplain of Worcefter. It is that of being accomplices in the *fpiritual murder* of proteftants, by excluding them from heaven, on account of their being infected with the contagion of HERESY. But how far are catholics concerned in the falvation of fuch, as are feparated from the communion of their church? Only as far as chriftian charity obliges them to pray, *that all man may be faved and come to the knowledge of the truth*. They find the concern of their own falvation, no eafy, or unimportant affair; and he who would not wifh to prevent the eternal lofs of a fellow creature, however intereft, refentment, or pride might feparate them in this life, *deferves not the name of a chriftian*.

As to the condemnation of heretics, and want of charity in catholicks in excluding them from eternal life, they are artifices which mifreprefentation has often ufed, to excite the clamour and indig-

indignation of the ignorant and unthinking; A LEGERDEMAIN TRICK of controvertifts, and anniverfary preachers; a trick, with which your two ecclefiaftical recanters amufe the public, *in order to intereft a proteftant community in their caufe*, and thereby palliate the breach of their vows, under the femblance of charity and benevolence.

BEFORE the church affembled her councils, the condemnation of error—the neceffity of FAITH, and rejection of HERESY, were enforced in the fcriptures. The apoftle, who, fpeaking of himfelf fays, *that he became all to all, in order to gain all to Chrift*, thought it no breach of charity to write in the following manner to Titus, *A man that is an heretic, after the firft and fecond admonition reject; knowing that he that is fuch, is fubverted, and finneth, being condemned of himfelf.* (Titus c. iii. v. 9. 10.) In proportion as errors fprung up, this rule has been invariably followed. " Religion," fays St. Auguftine, " is not to be fought for amongft
" the philofophers, fince they approve
" by their actions, the fame worfhip
" which they condemn by their wri-
" tings; nor amongft heretics, who
" have

"have no share in the sacraments of the
"church; nor among schismatics, who
"have separated themselves from her
"pale; nor amongst the Jews, who
"expect no reward from God but such as
"are temporal and transitory; *but only
"in the church universally spread throughout
"the earth*; which makes use of the
"errors of others, for her own good:
"She makes use of the pagans, as the
"matter of her works; of heretics, as
"a proof of the purity of her doctrine;
"of schismatics, as a mark of her stabi-
"lity; and of the Jews, as an evidence
"of her excellency. Thus, she invites
"the heathens; thrusts out heretics;
"forsakes schismatics; goes before the
"Jews; and yet she opens to all en-
"trance into the mysteries, and a door
"of grace; either by forming the faith
"of the former, or reforming the errors
"of the latter; or by causing the last
"to return to her bosom; or by ad-
"mitting others into the society of her
"children." Such are the sentiments
of St. Augustine, in his book *de Vera
Religione*: of him, who had been formerly
infected with the Manichean heresy, and
who, in his confessions, blames himself
for scorning to be a little one, in submit-
ting

ting to the paſtors of the church. And ſuch were the ſentiments of the primitive councils and fathers, who diſtinguiſhed the catholic faith from hereſy, and employed both their authority and talents, in ſupporting the firſt, and combatting the ſecond.

Let the charge of uncharitableneſs towards heretics, be brought againſt ſuch of the reformed churches as retain the Athanaſian creed, and againſt all antiquity, as well as againſt the catholic. Dr. Godolphin, a proteſtant canoniſt, in his Abridgement of the Eccleſiaſtical Laws of England, after Sir Edward Coke, calls hereſy " a leproſy of the ſoul;" and gives a catalogue of no leſs than one hundred and thirty-ſeven hereſies, condemned by the primitive church,* and what is *very remarkable* amongſt thoſe hereſies, he reckons that of Vigilantius, whom he calls, an apostate monk who condemned virginity, and againſt whom, as he remarks, St. Jerome wrote. The catholics of Worceſter may therefore judge on which ſide authority pre-

* See Godolphin's Repertorium Canonicum.

ponderates, and whofe doctrine is the purer; that of St. Jerome and the primitive fathers, who after St. Paul, recommend virginity; or that of MODERN CHAPLAINS, who after embracing VIRGINITY, by a folemn vow, equally violate both.

How groflly then is not the catholic mifreprefented by the outcry againft HERESY? as if it was to his uncharitablenefs, the odious term owed its rife. Nor are the ignorant lefs impofed on when the catholic is fingled out as the only *fpiritual mifanthrope*, who would have no enjoyment in heaven, if he faw a perfon of a different perfuaofin from his own within its gates. But let us examine with what juftice this charge is brought againft a Roman catholic, and whether he be the only unfociable TIMON, who carreffed none but ALCIBIADES, becaufe he expected he would be the caufe of the death of feveral, and gave warning to fuch of his fellow citizens as intended to hang themfelves, to make ufe of a tree in his garden before he cut it down. In a word, has a catholic fuch an intemperate averfion to the falvation of his proteftant neighbour, as the

the Scotch preacher had to the falvation *of Lawyers*, when he faid, "HELL was fo full of them, that none of his congregation could find room *there*."

To determine on the eternal lofs of a fellow creature, is a difagreeable office. And when the queftion is propofed, whether *an honeft man who has not the true faith will be damned*, it is painfull to me to become a cafuift. It is a tafk I would willingly refign to fome other; I, who declare in the moft folemn manner (were I to confult my own feelings, *as a man*, and not the rule of St. Paul, who declares that *without faith it is impoffible to pleafe God*), that if God lodged the keys of his palace in my hands, with full permiffion to admit whom I thought fit, I would not exclude one of Adam's children; no, not even the leader of the proteftant affociations LORD GEORGE GORDON, though he offered his URIEL SPEAR to the Dutch ambaffador, againft the KING OF THE ROMANS, and is fo devoutly inclined, *that no ftrumpet* ever difpleafed him, *except the ftrumpet of Babylon*,*

---

* *Nulla meretrix ipfi difplicuit preter meretricem Babylonicam.* A line in the epitaph of Sheppard the highwayman, equally famous for his *love for women*, as his

whether it be on account of the furrows which OLD AGE has traced in her cheeks, which doubtlefs muft give a difrelifh to a young man of his amorous complexion; or whether it be on account of the coftlinefs and magnificence of her drefs, which Jack, in *Swift's Tale of a Tub*, could not endure, but tore off with an unmerciful hand and forbade any the leaft fhred of it ever to be tacked to the fhort and fanctified jackets of levellers and round heads, or from whatever other caufe this *averfion* may proceed, his lordfhip himfelf can beft inform us.

Nor would I even exclude any of the *motley-group* of coblers, tinkers, draymen, link-boys, fcavengers, chimney fweepers, &c. &c. &c. &c. who met to the number of SIXTY THOUSAND in St. George's fields to reform the church of England, and the Britifh conftitution, however awkward the appearance they would make amongft the inhabitants of

---

his *hatred for popery*. The author of the hiftory of Lord North's adminiftration relates, that the ingenious Mr. Wilkes applied *this verfe* to LORD GEORGE when he faw him enter the houfe of commons with his *blue cockade* at the time of the *memorable riots*.

F   that

that Jerusalem above which is called THE CITY OF PEACE; for I am confident there is room enough for us all in its extensive mansions, and that when I got them within side the gates, they would immediately *change their manners.*

BUT what right have I to parcel out the kingdom of Heaven amongst my neighbours, whilst I have no infallible certainty that myself will ever possess the smallest corner of it; whereas the scripture says, that *no man knows whether he be worthy of love or hatred,* and that he alone *who endureth to the end will be saved.* The kingdom of heaven is not an easy purchase: it must be taken by violence: for if St. Paul, that vessel of election, who exhorts us *to work out our salvation with fear and trembling,* was under continual apprehensions left he should loose the precious treasure of sanctifying grace; if under this anxiety he requests the prayers of his brethren, *lest whilst in preaching to others himself might become a reprobate;* if he uses these alarming words, *I am conscious of nothing to myself, but in this I am not justified, for the Lord judgeth me;* with what security can we flatter ourselves? We, who to use his own words, *carry*

carry the treasure of grace in brittle glasses; We, who feel but a languid desire to reap an eternal harvest, yet take but little pains to sow and cultivate in time the prolific grain, and who daily and wilfully expose to the winds and storms of various temptations, that SACRED LAMP OF INNOCENCE, which was extinguished in the hands of the very virgins who neglected to supply it, with *the oil of vigilance and fervour.*

But still the question recurs: who are the persons excluded from salvation, and are heretics of the number? to which I answer, that the church does not, nor cannot exclude from happiness, or admit to salvation, but such as are excluded therefrom by the justice of God, or admitted thereto by his mercy: much less does she wish the loss of any one. She, who prays for all, that God would bring them *to the knowledge of the truth*, and crown them with eternal bliss. She knows that several go astray, and therefore prays for their conversion. But in believing that false doctrines, and bad morals, endanger the salvation of man, and in using her efforts to guard him against the danger, she is no more uncharitable, than a perſon who ſeeing another run to the brink of, what he thinks, *a precipice*, believes that his life is in danger, and *cautions him* againſt the fall.

Wɪᴛʜ regard to eternal life, and the requiſites towards its attainment, we could know but little without the aid of revelation. How could we imagine that the effuſion of water on the body of an infant, attended with the utterance of a few words, could make him an adopted child of God, and heir to his kingdom? a ceremony, which when preſented on their ſtage, moved the heathens to laughter.

Oɴ the other hand, if we conſider reaſon as our only oracle, we ſhudder at the thought of ſo many calamities, temporal and eternal, entailed upon mortals in puniſhment of the diſobedience of one man, who taſted an apple; though we would conſider that maſter a bloody tyrant, who would deprive a ſlave of his life for ſuch a trifle; ſtill, are we uncharitable for believing the tranſgreſſion fion of one man will be the occafion of the lofs of feveral?

IN like manner, when Chrift declares in the fcriptures, that *who ever believeth not, will be condemned*; when St. Paul declares, *that an heretic is fubverted, and finneth, being condemned of himfelf*; when St. Peter declares, *that feveral pervert the facred writings to their own deftruction*; are we uncharitable for believing what is revealed? efpecially, when we wifh and pray that no perfon may bring deftruction on himfelf? if a catholic be uncharitable for believing thefe things, let not his creed, but the fcripture be blamed. He fees a Church eftablifhed, with repeated injunctions to believe and obey her; he reads the folemn promifes of her divine founder, whereby he binds himfelf *to direct and affift her to the end of time*; he reads that *God daily added to the church fuch as fhould be faved*; he fees that after the eftablifhment of this church, neither the rigid virtue of a SAUL, under the Jewifh difpenfation, of which God had been the author; nor the good works of *Cornelius the centurion*, the ftrict obferver of the law of nature, were deemed fufficient until they become members of the

the church, to which " God daily added
" fuch as fhould be faved :" He fees a
caution given by Chrift againft falfe
prophets, *who would appear in fheep's cloathing*; and by St. Paul againft fuch of the
chriftians themfelves, *as would fay perverfe things to draw difciples after them*; he
fees the children of the church grown
up under the care of their paftors, feeding them with the doctrine of truth,
before the abortives of error and herefy
made their appearance; thofe abortives
rejected and difowned, as a *fpurious offspring*; all innovations in matters of
doctrine immediately oppofed; *nihil innovatur*, and a ftanding rule laid down by
the fathers, " that whoever expects to
" have GOD for his FATHER muft have
" THE CHURCH for his MOTHER," a rule,
fo well known to heathen writers, that
PORPHYRY, the mortal enemy of chriftians, perceiving fo many fects amongft
them in his time, diftinguifhes between
the doctrines of thofe fectaries, and that
of what he calls τον εκκλησιαν μεγαλην, or
THE GREAT CHURCH. Upon fuch authorities, he believes the danger of error.
Candour and common fenfe muft acknowledge, that I am not uncharitable
for feeing a perfon mifs the road, which

I be-

I believe to be the right one, when I am inclined to lead him into the fafeſt path, if he takes me for his guide.

STILL, we are to diſtinguiſh the firſt broachers of error, from the children, and grand children of thoſe whom they ſeduced; either by dazzling them with their eloquence, or moving their paſſions, or alluring them with the attractive bait of temporal intereſt. Whether hereſy, according to the compilers of Lexicons, ſignifies *choice*, when a perſon chuſes a wrong religion; or whether it ſignifies *diviſion*, when a perſon divides from the unity of the faith, which according to St. Auguſtine happens either from unconquerable pride, diſorderly paſſions, temporal intereſt or THE LOVE OF SENSUAL PLEASURES; whether hereſy, I ſay, ſignifies choice or diviſion, it implies wilful obſtinacy. The firſt broachers of it are thoſe againſt whom, in every age, the cenſures of eccleſiaſtial authority were chiefly directed; in conformity with the rule of St. Paul, *reject an heretic after the firſt or ſecond admonition, for ſuch is condemned of himſelf.* They were the firſt who made the choice, and divided from unity, their errors were their own

own, and *wilful*; but when once their errors are eſtabliſhed—ſupported by the laws of temporal princes—confirmed by time, and ſanctioned by the multitude, however criminal they might have been in the firſt authors and their adherents, yet with regard to ſucceeding generations, they become hereditary, and for the moſt part *involuntary:* And here we muſt incline as much as poſſible to the ſide of charity; without becoming *latitudinarians* on the one hand, or removing *the ſacred land mark*, which Chriſt and his apoſtles have ſet up, on the other.

ALL perſons who are baptized "have the baptiſm of the church," ſays St. Auguſtine, let the religion of their parents or the perſon who confers it, be what it may, they become children of the church by baptiſm; they receive at their regeneration, the ſupernatural and habitual gifts of FAITH, HOPE and CHARITY; and as the gifts of God are permanent by their nature, whereas he never recals his favours till we render ourſelves unworthy of their continuance, the above virtues remain in the ſoul, till we forfeit them, either by the wilful blindneſs of the mind, or the criminal corruption of the heart

heart. Hence numbers are members of the church, unknown to themſelves; and on the ſuppoſition that ſuch perſons had not the opportunity of being inſtructed, or that their hearts were ſincere and that they preſerved their baptiſmal innocence, which is no eaſy matter during a long life, conſidering the weakneſs of nature and the corruption of the world, they certainly will be ſaved; and the catholic church has never declared otherwiſe. For by baptiſm on the foregoing ſuppoſition, they are her children not only unknown to themſelves who, from prejudices of education and invincible ignorance, rail againſt her, but alſo unknown to herſelf, as preſumption and outward appearances are againſt them; for it is agreed on all hands THAT INVINCIBLE IGNORANCE EXCUSES FROM SIN; *Non tibi deputatur ad culpam, quod invitus ignoras:* For, as Chriſt himſelf has declared, *that much will be required of him to whom much is given*; conſequently leſs will be required of the perſon to whom leſs is given. However we may pity or blame the change which their anceſtors have brought about, yet with regard to themſelves,

G we

we can apply Ovid's lines on Acteon, who incurred the difpleafure of Diana.

" And yet confider what the change has wrought,
" You'll find it a misfortune not a fault ;
" Or if a fault, it was the fault of chance,
" For how can *guilt* proceed from *ignorance* ?"

METAMOR. BOOK 3.

SUCH are the dictates of nature; to which St. Auguftine, the moft enlightened of chriftian doctors has given his fanction, when he faid, that, 'Such
' as fupport falfe opinions without obfti-
' nacy, but are ready to renounce them
' when they difcover their errors, efpeci-
' ally, when they themfelves were not
' the firft broachers of them, but recei-
' ved them as a legacy from their pa-
' rents, who had either been feduced,
' or had fallen into error, *are not to be*
' *ranked among the hereticks.*' " Dixit
" quidem apoftolus Paulus, hereticum
" hominem devita, &c. Sed qui fenten-
" tiam fuam, quamvis falfam atque
" perverfam, nulla pertinaci animofi-
" tate defendunt, prefertim, quum non
" audacia prefumptionis fuæ, fed a fe-
" ductis atque in errorem lapfis paren-
" tibus acceperunt, querunt cauta fol-
licit-

"licitudine veritatem, corrigi parati cum invenerint, nequaquam funt inter hereticos deputandi" (*St. Aug. Ep.* 43. *Editio. Lov.* 1614) It is not then the invincible ignorance of the truth, but the *wilful neglect* of enquiring after it, which renders a man *criminal*.

NUMBERS there are, who far from having an opportunity of being inftructed in the catholic doctrine, are taught from their very cradles to hate and deteft it; and if FAITH comes by *hearing*, it muft be acknowledged, that *error and mifreprefentation* are conveyed through *the fame channel*, and leave as deep an impreffion on the mind. In Scotland, where Knox and his difciples, whom the late Dr. Johnfon calls the *ruffians of the reformation*, and to whom Hume, though of a more refined polifh than Johnfon, does not pay more courtly compliment; in Scotland, I fay, where Knox and his fellow labourers have fown the feeds of eternal hatred, even againft *proteftant epifcopacy*, what chance has the lower clafs of knowing any thing tending to recommend the catholic religion? when they are taught to believe that the Pope has *horns*, and, if

if we may credit Jacob Curate, that bishops have *cloven feet?* such disciples have more to dread from a breach of the moral law, than from error in matters of doctrine; at least while they have no other catechisms, or teachers, than those to whom they have been hitherto accustomed; and although St. Jerome, in his Epistle to Pope Damascus, amidst the theological disputes which distracted the east in his time, declares, " That he " adheres to St. Peter's chair, and who" ever eats the pascal lamb out of this " temple, is profane;" so I declare it is my belief, that the male and female disciples of a Scotch parson, will be more answerable for deserving to be seated on the stool of repentance, on which it is said these young fanatics are exposed in the congregation of saints for indulging the affection of the sexes (*though they think it meritorious to burn the houses of their catholic neighbours*) than for their separation from the center of unity; which they are persuaded to be the seat of antichrist. Hence, no Roman catholic divine in taking his degrees, ever swears he believes that a protestant will be damned. He swears to hold and believe, what is held and believed by the
Roman

Roman catholic and apoſtolic church, which has never defined that a perſon baptized in the chriſtian religion, reared up in hereditary and involuntary error, remote from the means and opportuntiy of inſtruction, and preſerving their baptiſmal innocence, will die in a ſtate of reprobation. She thinks otherwiſe of perſons who know the truth, and from *worldly motives* will not embrace it. She thinks ſtill worſe of her *apoſtate children*, who after being nurſed up, and inſtructed in her boſom, *quit her pale*, which Saint Jerome calls Noah's Ark, out of which whoever ſeeks for ſhelter, *muſt periſh by the Deluge.* " Si quis in " Arca Noæ non fuerit, peribit, regnante " Diluvio." But ſhe thinks worſe of all of her APOSTATE MINISTERS, who after having profaned her altars and myſteries, and *ſullied* with the ſmoak of their paſſions *the pillars of her ſanctuary,* which the piety and chaſtity of their lives *ſhould have brightened,* trample on their ſacred vows, and like the *raven* in the ſcriptures, QUIT THE ARK to faſten on *carcaſſes.* To ſuch, without any breach of charity, ſhe can apply the words of St. Paul, " If we have wilfully " ſinned after we have received the " knowledge

" knowledge of the truth, there re-
" maineth but a certain fearful looking
" for judgment, and a fiery indigna-
" tion." *Voluntarie præcantibus, jam non relinquitur hoſtia* (Heb. c. x. v. 36.) Neither is it a breach of charity in her, but rather the effect of charity, to be anxious for the ſalvation of ſuch as are out of her pale; becauſe ſhe believes there is but ONE FAITH, and knows that *errors are without number.*

IT is not ſafe to follow falſe guides who ſay, *Lo Chriſt is here! and Chriſt is there!* for if the heathen philoſophers, from the very nature of man, who is apt to err various ways, require two things in order to live aright, viz. to *know* what ſhould be done, and when known *readily to perform it*; is it not more incumbent on the Chriſtian, *who is exalted above his nature*, to uſe every effort *to come to the knowledge* of the TRUE FAITH, and when known, *readily to embrace it?*

MOREOVER, as ſhe believes a ſacrament of regeneration, requiſite for infants on account of the ſtain they contract by an others guilt; ſo likewiſe does ſhe believe a ſacrament of reconciliation, requiſite
for

for the adult, who as often as they sin, contract so many stains of their own; for lapses are frequent, and almost universal. She believes that with her the remedy is deposited. She pities those who are remote from, or reject her assistance. And tho' it is impossible to determine the fate of every Christian, as God alone can know the measure of grace—the degree of knowledge—the sufficiency or insufficiency of the means of information conferred on him, yet she considers as *dangerous*, the state of such as live and die *out of her communion*, because she believes herself in possession of *the means* of their sanctification—the true faith—the real priesthood—the altar—the sacrifice of atonement—the sacrament of reconciliation—and the power of the keys. Such being the case, is the Church more blameable than the physican who declares his opinion, that his patient is *in danger*; when at the same time he is both ready and willing to administer every remedy in his power *for his recovery?*

But what surprises me most of all is, that the charge of uncharitableness should be brought against the catholics of of England, where every candidate for any employment in church or state, from the ARCHBISHOP to the *parish sexton*; and from the ERMINED JUDGE to the *shabby catchpole*, is bound to swear, if not in express terms, at least by implication, *the damnation* of every Roman catholic on the face of the earth.

To what purpose the declaration, preceded by the solemnity of an oath, that the sacrifice of the mass, such as it is celebrated by the church of Rome, is *idolatrous* and superstitious; if not to impress the minds of the swearers with the belief, that the votaries of that church are IDOLATORS: and if damnation is to be distributed with a liberal hand, in the sunshine of revelation and after the promulgation of the gospel, who are the better intitled to the largest share of the *fatal gift*, than IDOLATORS?

WHAT noise in England, when Hooker, the author of Ecclesiastical Polity, had the charity to say in his discourse on justification, that he doubted *not but thousands of the fathers who lived and died in the superstitions of the church of Rome were saved*, because of their ignorance,
which

which excufeth them. The pious mafter, Walter Traverfe, was fo fhocked at this horrid doctrine, that he fent his fupplication to the privy council againft mafter Hooker, and afferts, *that fuch as die, or have died at any time in the church of Rome, holding in their ignorance that faith which is taught in it, cannot be faid by the fcriptures to be faved.**

Whoever could undergo the drudgery of fhading all the anniverfary Philippics againft popery, fince *the contrivance of Cecil*, one of the moft artful fchemers that England gave birth to, which has been honoured with a folemn feftival under the famous title of the GUNPOWDER PLOT, muft either acknowledge, that the preachers of fuch difcourfes have made an *horrid ufe* of their miniftry, or that it is as difficult for a catholic to enter the kingdom of Heaven, " as it is " for a camel to pafs through the eye of " a needle." This is what Pool, the author of the Synopfis, acknowledges in his Dialogues between a Papift and Proteftant.

* See Walter Traverfe's Supplication, at the end of Hooker's Eccl. Polity.

TILLOTSON, who for his zeal against popery, forgets now and then the dignity of the pulpit, *where irony is always misplaced,* however applicable it may be on other occasions; Tillotson, I say, is not much more lenient, when he inveighs against and ridicules, what Sheridan, the Author of the Rhetorical Grammar, calls, *that most ludicrous and detested religion* POPERY.

To the foregoing, we can add the long catalogue of protestant commentators on the Revelations of St. John and the Epistle of St. Paul to the Thessalonians, who have consumed an immense quantity of paper and candles to afright old women with the notion that the Pope is ANTICHRIST, and Rome BABYLON; for, in the scriptures, Christ and his apostles are put in opposition with Antichrist and his followers. The latter are no doubt excluded from salvation, as having the *marks of the beast*: and when I talk of those commentators, what clouds of witnesses could not I produce against the title which a Roman catholic may claim to the kingdom of heaven; from the *visions* of Mede on the Revelations down to bishop Newton's *Reveries* on the Prophets.

DOCTOR

DOCTOR WATSON, at present regius professor of divinity at Cambridge, cannot defend the cause of christianity in a few letters to Mr. Gibbon, author of the Decline and Fall of the Roman Empire, without searing the consciences of Roman catholics with a hot iron, and branding them with the *characteristical marks* of the votaries of the *man of sin*, "Whom the "Lord is to consume with the spirit of "his mouth, and destroy with the "brightness of his coming," *because they do not eat meat on Fridays.*

IN answer to Mr. Gibbon's remark on the belief of the primitive christians concerning the time of the last judgment, Mr. Watson leaps from the epistle of St. Paul to the Thessalonians, wherein the apostle speaks of the last judgment and of Antichrist, who about that time is to make his appearance, to St. Paul's epistle to Timothy, whom he cautions against the false doctrines of the Simoneans, Marceonites, &c. forbidding *to marry and abstain from meats*; because those heretics, according to the primitive ecclesiastical

* See Watson, page 40, or the whole of his enthusiastical rhapsody, from page 33 to 43.

writers, considered marriage and the flesh *as the works of the devil.* The same writers inform us in like manner, that some of those heretics, especially the SIMONEANS, held that *it was not God,* but the demons, or angels, *that created the world:* a doctrine which St. Paul might with propriety have called *the doctrine of devils;* because it was *false.* But Mr. Watson proves from Newton, that it is the canonization of saints.

LIKE Sterne, in his *Tria juncta in uno,* he jumbles the different chapters and different subjects into one context, to prove that catholics are the *adopted children* of Antichrist. He then lays down rules which furnishes every deist with an argument which saps the foundation of revealed religion, by informing the world, that the apostles followed their own understandings, when they had no other light to guide them; *speaking from conjecture* (says he) *when they could not speak from certainty of themselves, when they had no commandment from the Lord.*‡ Thus he explains away the difficulties stated by Mr. Gibbon—*n'importe*—St. Paul, there-

‡ Page 42.

fore,

fore, either marks out the catholics as members of Antichrift, or he *did not know what he was faying*; tho' St. Paul declares, in that very epiftle, that *he fpoke by the word of the Lord.* By Mr. Watfon's rule, he makes himfelf a greater prophet than St. Paul: for according to him, St. Paul fpoke *from conjecture*; but in attributing to the catholics *confciences feared with a hot iron, the doctrine of devils, &c.* and confequently the *punifhment* due to fuch *abominations,* Mr. Watfon *fpeaks from certainty.*

THE charge of uncharitablenefs therefore can be eafily retorted; and if the denial of falvation to thofe whom we deem in error, be fufficient ground for the accufation, we can fay with the poet, *Iliacos intra muros & extra.* The Athanafian Creed contains *a damnatory claufe,* which thoufands who profefs themfelves chriftians, abhor and difrelifh; it is as incumbent therefore on the proteftant prelates and doctors who fubfcribe to it, *to reconcile it with the rules of charity,* as it is on the Roman catholics.

To this charge, the Chaplain adds that other fo often repeated, and as much mifunderftood as the former, viz. *the unwarrantablenefs of impofing the law of celibacy on the clergy.* The church never *forces* celibacy upon her minifters, but *cancels* and difannuls *all vows,* which are made *from force, or fraud.* It is true fhe *opens* her fanctuary to the candidates for ordination, upon certain conditions; but fhe rejects the man who *enters it with reluctance.* The alternative is at their own *free choice,* either to become her minifters, and lead a life of *celibacy,* or to fanctify themfelves in the world in a ftate of *marriage.* She takes every precaution to try their vocation; points out to them the fanctity and obligations of the ftate they are going to embrace; and never ordains them, till they attain to the age, when the impulfe of paffion is fufficiently felt; and when they fhould know, how far they have power and inclination to refift them. It is then in confequence of their own free choice, and the *deliberate vows* they make to the Almighty, that they *are bound to celibacy.* If they find the yoke which they impofe on themfelves for the fake of Jefus Chrift *too heavy,* let them blame their

want

want of prayer—fervour—and vigilance; for God being every where prefent to call them to his fervice—to comfort them in their hopes—confirm them in his love---help their endeavours—and to hear their prayers, they are under *no impoffibility* of refifting their lufts and paffions. Amidft the temptations of the world and furrounded by a variety of objects to which the catholic clergy, from the ftraitnefs and gravity of their profeffion, are not expofed, widows, widowers, unmarried people of both fexes in the bloom and vigour of youth, and married perfons during a long abfence from each other, are bound to live chafte and fpotlefs, and to refift their lufts and paffions.

THE provofts and fellows of feveral proteftant univerfities, are *bound to celibacy* whilft they intend to continue in their ftations, or partake of the immunities and privileges of their refpective profeffions. Doctor Mann, the proteftant bifhop of the diocefe in which I refide, is now almoft a feptuagenary, and never married. Many proteftant clergymen of my acquaintance, are in the fame ftate, after having gone through life with an unfullied reputation, and are

as

as watchful in curbing their paſſions, as if they made the ſame vow by which I am bound. But is not marriage free? It is: and for which reaſon the clergy of other religions *do not ſin in marrying,* becauſe they have *not made a vow* to the contrary. Neither does the number of their ſacraments—rites—functions— or ceremonies require ſo ſtrict a ſeceſſion from worldly affairs and the embarraſſments attending the ſupport of a wife and children, as is required from a catholic clergyman, if he attends to, or acquits himſelf as he ought of his duty. But did the clergy of other perſuaſions, *make a ſolemn vow* to the Almighty, I am confident that the *conſcientious* amongſt them, would *ſcruple to break it.*

Saint Paul, in his firſt epiſtle to the Corinthians, chap. the 7th, declares, that marriage and celibacy are left to our free choice: though he gives the preference to the latter, on account of the reaſons alleged in that chapter; reaſons *very applicable* to the miniſters of the altar. But as Hooker, in his Eccleſiaſtical Polity, and ſeveral other proteſtant divines, judiciouſly remark, *the indifferency of choice is removed, by a ſupervening tye*
or

or bond. " This indifferency is removed," *says Hooker*, " If we either take away our
" own liberty, as Ananias did, for
" whom to have fold or held his pof-
" feſſion it was indifferent, till the
" *ſolemn vow and promiſe made to God* had
" ſtrictly bound him one only way."*

THE Nazarites, in like manner, could have *ſhaved their heads and drank wine* without guilt; had they not bound themſelves to *abſtemiouſneſs and auſterity of dreſs*. The heathens themſelves were ſtruck with ſuch *awe*, at the ſolemnity of the obligations contracted with the gods, that *death itſelf* could ſcarce atone for the *incontinency* of their veſtals. But when I read of a pagan REGULUS voluntarily encountering the moſt cruel tortures in compliance with the *oath* he had made on the *profane altars* of Carthage, I am more inclined *to bluſh*, than argue, when I ſee the miniſters of the TRUE GOD ſport with the vows whereby they bound themſelves *irrevocably* to his ſervice.——I am aſhamed to ſee the ſame perſon, who was *chaſte* at the age of twenty-four, become *lewd* at the age of

* Book 2d. page 109.

thirty-

thirty-five, or forty. When I fee *the jewifh priefts themfelves* bound to abftain from the marriage bed during the time of their miniftration in the temple; I tremble with *a chilling horror* at the fight of PRIESTS OF THE NEW LAW, accuftomed from their early days, *to the purity and chaftity* becoming their function, and ftrengthened by the fanctity of a SOLEMN VOW to God in the face of his altars, *renounce thier allegiance* to HIM who fays, " That fome make them-
" felves eunuchs for the kingdom of
" heaven," and after putting their hands to the plough, *look back*, and lift under *the banners* of Epicurus.

THE celibacy of the clergy, as I have obferved before, is the refult of their own *free* and deliberate *choice*. Should any amongft them therefore *violate* the indifpenfible obligations voluntarily impofed on themfelves by *a folemn vow*, the blame muft be attributed to their own mifconduct——diffipation——want of prayer—fervour—vigilance—and their neglect to *avoid* the dangerous occafions of fin, to which, whoever expofes himfelf, *will infallibly fall*; for according to the gofpel maxim, " Whoever loves the
" danger,

" danger, shall perish therein." Let their converfation and actions therefore tend to the *edification*, not the *feduction* of the other fex. Let them call to mind, that as the TENDER ROSE is guarded by the SURROUNDING THORNS, fo the *delicacy* of the CLERICAL VOWS muft be protected by THE FENCES OF PRAYER, MORTIFICATION AND VIGILANCE. In a word: let them remember, that according to Saint Bernard, " *a trifle* in a layman is often " *a profanation* in a clergyman;" and that after having devoted themfelves to God by a folemn vow, their only fafe guard is, a ftrict adherence to the maxim of St. Paul, " Let every man abide " *in the fame calling* wherein he was " called." (1ft Ep. Cor. 7th chap.) Let them reflect that the faith of compacts and promifes is fo *inviolable*; that it binds man to man, *even to an enemy*—— that no arguments fuggefted *by flesh and blood*, can juftify the breach of a promife made to GOD, the *beft and moft generous of friends*; and that the catholic clergymen, *who violate their vows of chaftity*, fhould they publifh APPEALS to fcripture, &c. in *vindication* of their conduct, or even ten folios of controverfy, are to be ranked amongft THE HERD OF EPI-

CURUS's

curus's swine, *inter porcos gregis Epicuri.* In which fraternity I shall leave them, and conclude with a short remark on Dr. Carroll's Address, for TROJANS or TYRIANS are alike to me, only as far as they deviate from, or adhere to, what I esteem, THE TRUTH. A few days ago, a gentleman, who landed here from America presented me with Dr. *Carroll's Address,* in an answer to Mr. *Wharton's Letter.* The only difference I find between the London and Anapolis editions of this address, is, the POSTSCRIPT, already mentioned—the editor's manner of arranging and condensing the doctor's arguments, whereby they become more clear and perspicuous to the reader, and the omission of a NOTE ‡, in which the doctor attributes the downfal of the society of which he was once a member, to *the unworthy condescension, and sinister views, of an artful and temporising pontiff* (GANGANELLI.)

‡ To indulge the curiosity of the public, the editor has inserted the note above mentioned in the preface to the second edition of Dr. Carroll's Address, after stating *the motives* which induced him to suppress it, in the first edition,

As to poſtſcripts, annotations, &c. to the works of others, there is nothing more uſual amongſt editors: and when the author of the poſtſcript ſays, *The catholics of Worceſter are inclined to believe that the motives of their late chaplain's converſion did not originate in* DIVINE LOVE, he only attributes to them an opinion, founded on the experience of ages; and which the chaplain himſelf has confirmed in expreſs terms by aſſerting, in the ſeventeenth page of his letter, that he conſidered the chaſtity to which he had bound himſelf, " as a cruel uſurpa-
" tion of the unalienable RIGHTS OF
" NATURE; as *unwarrantable* in its prin-
" ciple, *inadequate* in its object, and
" *dreadful* in its conſequences." That Mr. H-k-n's in his pamphlet entitled A FEW REMARKS ON DOCTOR CARROLL'S ADDRESS, ſhould appear no leſs *nettled* at the poſtſcript, than at the editor's manner of arranging the ſeveral points of controverſy under their *reſpective titles* and diſtinguiſhing *certain paſſages* by the introduction of SMALL CAPITALS or *italics*, as their dignity or force ſeemed to require; that Mr. H---, I ſay, who ſtands *exactly* in the ſame predicament with the chaplain, ſhould find the *delicacy*

cacy of his feelings so much wounded by such *typographical illustrations*, is by no means paradoxical, or surprising, when we consider that by such *auxiliaries*, the force of the doctor's arguments acquire *additional strength*, and make *a deeper impression* on the mind of the reader. To correct, arrange, or illustrate such errors, paragraphs or passages as escape the attention of authors or printers, is, not only the undoubted privilege, but the *indispensible duty* of editors *, under this restriction, however,

---

* The following are specimens of the ungrammatical passages which, either through the negligence of the printer, or inattention of the author in revising the proof sheets, have crept into the Anapolis edition of Dr. Carroll's Address, and which the London editor found himself under the necessity of correcting. " And *the church*, ever guided by the spirit of " God, sees when the dangers threatening her chil- " dren from false prophets, arising and seducing " many, *call upon her* to examine the faith commit- " ted *to her* keeping, &c." (p. 52. An. Edit.) in order to do away the absurdity *of the church's calling upon herself*, the foregoing passage stands thus corrected in the London Edition. " The children *of* " *the church ever guided by the spirit of God*, seeing " the dangers threatening them from false prophets " arising and seducing many, call *upon her* to deli- " ver the faith committed *to her* keeping, &c." here the natural connexion between the *children of the church*, viz. the faithful, and the *church herself*, is re-

restored;

that they do not *alter* the sense of the author; of this the editor of Doctor Carroll's Address cannot be accused; for after comparing his, with the Anapolis edition, I find *the cloath to be the same*, he has only given it a *smarter trim*, and the tighter THE JACKET OF CONTROVERSY, the better.

stored; by representing them, as *calling upon her* to declare the faith committed to her charge, in opposition to the dangers threatening them from false prophets, arising and seducing many.

Again, p. 89. 90. " The heathens *may* have ob-
" jected—the mystery of the incarnation, &c.—they
" *may* have grounded on the christian doctrine of
" redemption, &c.—they *may*, from the examples it
" offorded them, &c.—they *may* have availed them-
" selves, &c." Here the word MAY, in speaking of the disputes which subsisted between the primitive Christians and their heathen cotemporaries so many ages ago, is substituted in four several places in the same paragraph, instead of MIGHT; whereas the former implies either the present or future, and the latter the preterite or past tense, to which time the above passages evidently refer. For these, and other corrections of less moment, but more especially for the annexed Postscript, the cancelled note, &c. already mentioned by Mr. O'Leary, the London edition is stigmatized with the epithets, *rent and mangled*, by the *editor* of an edition printed at Worcester, because the editor thereof has not, like *himself*, servily copied all the errors and inaccuracies of the Anapolis edition.

THE

THE CANCELLED NOTE, reflecting on Ganganelli, was an *unseemly patch*, ill matched to the quality and colour *of the suit*, which the Chaplain and Doctor Carroll exposed for the inspection of the public. It was *a digression*, quite unconnected with the *main subject* in debate; the insertion of which would prove more injurious to the dead, than instructive to the living: Had the two authors handled their subject in *a poetical strain*, Ganganelli's character, and the fall of the society of which they were both formerly members, might be brought in by the way of an EPISODE. Fictions in poetry may be excused: but that Ganganelli was *artful or designing*, or that the Jesuits *fell victims to his sinister views*, is, a FICTION of which I cannot suppose a gentleman of Doctor Carroll's character to be the original fabricator.

Ganganelli was neither artful nor designing; if he had the *wisdom of the serpent*, he had also the *simplicity of the dove:* nor was he of so flexible and temporising a disposition, as to be awed into any measure, contrary to justice and conscience. He, who wrote to one of the greatest kings

kings in Europe when preſſed to a meaſure to which he could not *reconcile his conſcience,* " That he would not get in- " ſide the threſhold of hell, for all the " kings on the face of the earth." Neither was it his intereſt, nor the intereſt of mankind, let politicians ſay what they will, *to aboliſh ſuch an illuſtrious body,* as the ſociety of the Jeſuits ; who *civilized* ſo many barbarous nations—diffuſed *the light of the goſpel* into remote regions, whither the ALEXANDERS or CÆSARS had never carried their arms——contributed ſo extenſively *to the culture of the ſciences,* for in what branch of them *did they not excel? realized* in the very centre of barbariſm, amongſt cannibals feeding on each others fleſh, *the ſublime ideas* of a Plato, a Sir Thomas More, or a Fenelon; who only *dreamt* of theſe political eſtabliſhments, in which man could *live happy,* without the canker of *envy,* or the ſting of *poverty,* and RAISED THIS FABRIC, which has procured them the compliments of a Montiſquieu, and excited THE ADMIRATION OF MANKIND! It was not *the intereſt,* much leſs *the inclination* of Ganganelli, to deprive the catholic ſchools of the moſt *learned and edifying*

K *profeſſors*

professors—savage nations, of the moſt *zealous and active miſſionaries*—the chriſtian pulpits, of the *greateſt orators*—the very apoſtolical ſee, of the moſt *ſtrenuous aſſertors* of its privileges—or the ſciences, of their moſt *ſucceſsful and improving votaries.*

At the time of this unexpected affair, I was not far from the ſcene, in which the policy of ſtateſmen, and the power and intereſt of the prieſthood, played their reſpective parts. I had every opportunity of information, on account of my being honoured with the acquaintance of cardinal de Luines, then archbiſhop of Sens, chief almoner to the queen of Lewis the XVth, and Ganganelli's great friend; beſides ſeveral other occaſions. I was the more deſirous of being acquainted with every tranſaction, as when I ſaw my neighbours houſe threatened with the flames, I began to tremble for my own. *Paximus ardet Ucalegon.*

Ganganelli uſed every effort to diſperſe *the ſtorm*, which was every day approaching to *a vertical point*, over the ſociety's fociety's head. When he found three years delay and intreaties ineffectual, he propofed *a perfonal confrence* with the king at Avignon; which being refufed, he propofed *to convene a general council*, in prefence of which, the Jefuits fhould have *full l.berty to juftify themfelves*, and anfwer the charges of their adverfaries. But every exertion in their behalf *proving abortive*, he was at laft obliged *to yield to the torrent* and abolifh one fociety of men, in order to prevent a greater evil, which would probably be *the fchifm* of feveral kingdoms, or a continual *ftate of diftraction* in which, the very end of the Jefuits inftitution *would be defeated*, as the crowned heads began to banifh them from their dominions, in which they taught and inftructed with fuch edification for the fpace of almoft three hundred years.

ALL canonifts agree, that in emergencies lefs critical, it is in the power of the fovereign pontiff *to diffolve religious o ders*. They are aggregate bodies under their own peculiar rules and inftitutions—but their *charter* is under *the control* of the SUPREME HEAD, who is invefted vested by the church with *the power of annulling or confirming it*, according to the emergencies of times and places. The *dissolution* of the Jesuits then, was owing to *their influence*, which rendered them objects of envy *to artful ministers of state*, whose ambitious projects they often controlled as directors of monarchs, and members of their spiritual councils. It was owing to the expectation of *immense wealth*, with which kings themselves were flattered, by *the abolition of the order*. And tho' they have been disappointed in their expectations, yet, what will not crowned heads undertake, when pressed by the AURI SACRA FAMIS! And although the Jesuits proved their innocence against the charges of their adversaries in their work entitled *Appel a la Raison*, or *an Appeal to Reason*, yet what will innocence avail before an *earthly tribunal*, where crowned heads become *accusers*, and reserve to themselves *the right* to pronounce sentence?——In such case, the *pontiff's censure*, is but a weak defence against *the power of confederate monarchs*, for useless *stiffness* must yield to useful *prudence*.

No perfon can blame doctor Carroll's feelings at the difagreeable recollection of the fall of an illuftrious fociety of which he had been a member. But Ariftotle's rule is invariably to be followed, " If Plato be dear to me, *truth is dearer.*" Abbe de Matzel, one of the moft celebrated Jefuits of Bavaria, in his funeral oration on Ganganelli, is far from attributing to him any *finifter views.* And the more celebrated father de Neuville, whofe eloquence had fuch charms for lord Chefterfield, recommended at his death a refpect incapable of belying itfelf, towards the holy fee, and the pontiff who filled it. Contrary to the ordinary courfe of things, what was moft likely to give permanency to the order, was *the very caufe* of the downfal of the Jefuits; viz. their great credit, power and authority. They have literally verified the remark of Tacitus, *that eminent virtue, is liable to envy.* " Siniftra " erga eminentes interpretatio, nec minus " periculum ex magna fama, quam ex " mala." Candour and truth will, I hope, hereafter induce doctor Carroll to afcribe the fall of his fociety to the foregoing caufes, and not the *finifter views of* of a *pontiff*, whom Europe has revered, and whose memory will be tranſmitted to future ages, IN CHARACTERS OF IM- MORTALITY.

I remain, Sir,

Your affectionate

Humble ſervant,

Cork, January 6, 1786.

ARTHUR O'LEARY.

A

LETTER FROM CANDOUR

TO THE

Right Honourable LUKE GARDINER;

On his Bill for the Repeal of a Part of

𝕮𝖍𝖊 𝕻𝖊𝖓𝖆𝖑 𝕷𝖆𝖜𝖘

Againſt the IRISH CATHOLICS.

INTRODUCTION.

AFTER the catholics of Ireland had given the moſt unequivocal proofs of their loyalty and firm attachment to his Majeſty's perſon and government, it was reſolved, not only to exonerate them from a part of the grevious burthen of penal ſtatutes, which they had ſo long, and ſo patiently borne; but likewiſe to inveſt them with ſuch civil and religious privileges, as their own virtues and conduct, as ſubjects and citizens, had merited on the one hand; and the political intereſts of the Britiſh empire in general, ſeemed *loudly to demand*, on the other. For this purpoſe Mr. Gardiner was ordered to bring THE BILL, which is the ſubject of the following Letter, into THE IRISH HOUSE OF COMMONS; which, as it contained ſeveral clauſes, ill ſuited to the genius of *a liberal and enlightened age*, was as ſeverely cenſured cenfured by the moft refpectable members of that honourable houfe, as by the candid part of the nation at large.

The *fublime and beautiful author* of a fmall pamphlet lately publifhed on this fubject,* with that philanthropic fpirit which marks his character as the *ftrenuous advocate* of a depreffed people, how different foever their fentiments in religion may be from his own, points out feveral inftances wherein Mr. Gardiner's bill is, not only oppofite to the principles of humanity, but likewife inconfiftent with the maxims of found policy. And our author, whofe feelings as a catholic ecclefiaftic were roufed by fuch of its *obnoxious claufes* as he apprehended might hereafter operate to the prejudice of his religion, *remonftrates againft them* with the firmnefs of a Tertullian in the following manly and fpirited *apology*.

* Entitled, A Letter from a distinguished English Commoner to a Peer of Ireland, on the Repeal of a Part of the Penal Laws againft the Irifh Catholics.

A LETTER

A LETTER, &c.

SIR!

EVERY veneration, every respect, is due to a gentleman who is the first, in the long period of an hundred years, to take a few links from the heavy chain of bondage. Had you lived in antient times, and stept in to the relief of two millions of your fellow subjects, those states, which decreed the civic crown as a reward for preserving the life of a citizen, would have erected statues in your honour, and eternized your memory. A more glorious monument is erected in the breasts of the catholics of this kingdom, as well for you, as for those gentlemen who have supported, and are still inclined to support, the cause of humanity. This is not the language of adulation. Gratitude prompts——Truth dictates.

The liberty I shall take in the course of this letter, of passing my opinion on a part of your bill, exculpates me from the imputation of flattery.

With regard to the whole complex of the bill, I leave it to the discussion of other writers, who have taken up the subject—let them canvass it thoroughly. The voice of the public is, that the catholics of this kingdom deserve a great deal more——That people of property, whether real or personal, should have arms to defend it; whereas the plunderer of other people's property, the assassin, the robber, will have arms, maugre every prohibition. Penal laws are restraints on the honest, the virtuous, the industrious. No laws can bind the profligate. The general voice is, that the bar—the army—the navy—the revenue—should be thrown open to the votaries of every religion, according to their merit. That more effectual means should be taken, in order to diffuse a spirit of exertion and vigour through the torpid mass of a languid and dejected community; and that by our quibbles, and on account of our difference in modes of worship, we should no longer refemble the two knights-errant who fought about a ftatue, the one part whereof was painted white, the other black, without difcovering their miftake until each was feverely wounded, and in the conflict, changed their direction.

THE general voice is, that if this folace be examined on the grounds of religion, *religion gives it its fanction* ; for, where does religion exclude the brave and virtuous from the rights of citizens and fubjects : if on found policy, *Wifdom* raifes her voice, and proclaims it *her offspring*.

BUT to come to the point which chiefly regards the fubject of this letter. In fo enlightened an age, it was little expected that the fanguinary laws of the Tudors or Stuarts, would be again revived—that a fincere confcience, however erroneous, would become the object of vindictive ftatutes——that the catholic clergy of this kingdom, who have exerted themfelves in times of danger and trouble, and deferved fo well of the community, fhould be fingled out as victims of flaughter in a land of liberty,

liberty, where chriftians of every denomination, as well as unbelievers, have the privilege of thinking and acting as they pleafe, provided they neither rob, fteal, murder, nor commit thofe crimes which fap the foundations of morality, or diffolve the bands of fociety, or that Mr. Gardiner's hand, which nature has formed for applying the balfam to the fore, fhould point out to the fanatic or the informer, the fcabbard, from which he is to draw, the rufty dagger of perfecution.

I do not talk here Sir, of the prohibition to have fteeples and bells; I would as foon and as fervently go to prayers at the found of an old horn, as if all the bells in the city were chiming. I am neverthelefs furprized, that fuch veftiges of gothic barbarity, or Turkifh fuperftition, as to preclude the rearing of fteeples, or the ufe of bells, could be traced in a civilized country; whereas, a multitude and variety of fpires, fteeples, minerets and proud fabrics, fupported by ftately columns and arches, are the greateft ornaments a city can have: befides the tafte for fculpture and architecture which fuch buildings
would

would produce—the number of ingenious artifans and workmen employed—materials confumed, and the convenience arifing on Sundays to houfekeepers and fervants, who would know to a minute, at the laft toll of the bell, when prayers would begin, and lofe lefs time, on account of the certainty of the hour.

I do not talk here of thefe *intermarriages* you would introduce between catholics and proteftants; fo far, they have my hearty approbation: for MARRIAGE is the great tye of fociety. The proteftant who marries my fifter, becomes my brother: both families become one, and upon every occafion acquire additional ftrength, by *this union*; hence thofe primitive laws which prohibited relations within certain degrees of kindred to intermarry, were founded as much in the wifdom of policy, as in reverence to religion. Perfons prohibited to intermarry with their relations, fued for connections with other families: thus fociety extended and became *more united*. So far the bill is good. But the *provifo*, which inflicts fevere penalties on *one party* relative to the education of children, *embitters the fweets of the connubial ties*. A child

child born of parents of different perſuaſions, becomes the partizan of one, before he can diſtinguiſh. Upon any diſpute that may ariſe concerning the meaning of this act, the affair is to be determined in chancery. Let the oracle of the law be ever ſo equitably inclined, he will be under the neceſſity of having recourſe to the *rule*, FAVORES SUNT AMPLIANDI. *In favourable matters, the law muſt bear a favourable and extenſive conſtruction:* the caſe will conſequently be decided in favour of the proteſtant parent, as it was in his, or her *favour*, the act was framed; and a catholic father who thinks himſelf in the right, muſt be A MUTE in the preſence of his children, without daring to catechiſe them for the ſpace of fourteen years: the ſame can be ſaid of the catholic mother. Moreover, as marriage is founded on an *equality*, why ſhould the marriage of a proteſtant and catholic be *valid*, when ſolemnized by a proteſtant clergyman, and *null* when celebrated by a catholic paſtor, ſince each ſhould have an equal juriſdiction over his own flock. This clauſe ſhould either be expunged, or undergo the following amendment. " Such marriage to be *valid*, whether
" cele-

" celebrated by a proteſtant, or catho-
" lic clergyman—the children to be
" reared up as their parents *think fit*,
" and be at liberty to follow and pro-
" feſs which of the two religions they
" like beſt." 'Tis probable they will copy after the parent who ſets *the beſt example*.

I do not talk of the clauſe about re-giſtering the popiſh clergy, though it wounds the feelings and delicacy of a man of honour. MORAVIANS, ANTINO-MIANS, SECEDARS, HERENHUTTERS, in a word, the preachers and teachers of innumerable ſects and claſſes of diſ-ſenting chriſtians, are not regiſtered. The Britiſh parliament in reſcuing the catholic clergy from the clutches of in-formers, did not ſubject them to ſuch humiliating formalities, but left them to themſelves, without medling with their beads, breviaries, juriſdiction, ordina-tion, or eccliſiaſtical polity. It was be-neath the dignity and wiſdom of that legiſlative body, to enter into the minutiæ of eccleſiaſtical regulations for a body of men who cannot acquire any advantage in a ſtate where the eſtabliſhed religion is different from their own, but the liberty of exercifing it *unmolifted*, and who, by their religious principles, cannot recognize any fpiritual jurifdiction in a lay tribunal.

IN civilized countries there are generally but three claffes of people regiftered; viz. *the proftitutes* in Rome and Leghorn, *the galley flaves* in Breft and elfewhere, and *the parifh beggars* in England. It is the good fortune of an IRISH ECCLESIASTIC to give rife to, and be promoted to the rank of *a fourth order of nobility*. This law was enacted in the gloomy times of perfecution, to the furprize, as well as fcandal of the humane. As the catholic clergy of this kingdom are a treacherous, obnoxious fet of beings, who have fworn to overturn the ftate, and place the Pretender on the throne, it is but juft to fufpend a label from their necks engraved with the words, *habet fœnum in cornu!* However, as a man's name is no crime, I have no further exception to the enrolment of their names and furnames.

BUT the principal, and moft extraordinary claufe of the bill, is now to be can-

canvassed. All the pains, penalties, transportation, &c. are revived against those ecclesiastics, who either *directly* or *indirectly* pervert any protestant to the popish religion. By these two words DIRECTLY or INDIRECTLY, what a field is there not opened to perjured witnesses—subtil lawyers—fanatical jurors, and sanguinary judges, if such may be found. If a reward were assigned to a man for healing a sore in another, *directly* or *indirectly*, the duellist, who in defiance of the laws thrusts his sword into his antagonist's breast, and by this means *cures him of an imposthume,* could sue for his fee; he cured him *indirectly* and without any design.

In the original act I do not recollect to have read the words, *directly* or *indirectly,* which Mr. Gardiner inserts in his. Gracious Heaven, Sir! *what kind of monster must not a catholic be supposed,* whereas, whoever embraces his religion, becomes that instant *an outlaw?*

According to the enumeration made some years ago by the Royal Society, there were SIXTY-FOUR different religions in the three kingdoms; that is to say,

double the number of *jarring sects*, as there are winds that blow from the thirty-two points of the mariner's compass. All these religions shift and veer as they think fit; and why not? *the liberty of thinking and chusing, is the inherent right of man.* A protestant lawyer, and methodist preacher, turned Quakers the other day at Waterford. I knew a catholic, who would fain secure his estate on the one hand, but could never digest the oath of abjuration on the other; he put on a broad brimmed hat, without cocks; a plain coat, with a few buttons; changed his dialect from *you* and *ye*, into THOU and THEE; went to the Quakers meeting, GROANED IN THE SPIRIT, and thus secured his property, without calling God to witness to what he could not believe. Suppose this man, or several besides, who in a state of health *disguise their religion* from worldly motives, took some serious thought *at that awful moment when the mask is to be torn off*, and sent for a clergyman, must an ecclesiastic who complies with the duties of his ministry be conveyed in a cart to the gallows, or transported like a common felon, for affording him his charitable assistance at that *critical juncture?* or
what

what does society gain, or how is it interested *in forcing him to die* in hypocrisy and despair?

Suppose one of those sectaries, whose religion consists in beating the bushes early on Sunday morning with a pole, *in hopes that the desired of all nations would appear to him*, conversed with a catholic clergyman who would explain his religion to him, and exchange his *pole* for a *popish prayer book*, must this clergyman be treated as an outlaw, for telling him his mind? or what does Ireland lose by *settling this enthusiast's brain*, and procuring him a sound sleep on Sunday, till about eleven o'clock? whereas this sleep, besides refreshing him after his week's labour, will give him new strength and vigour for the work of the ensuing day.

Sixy-four different religions, some of which deny baptism itself, and thousands of *unbelievers* who consider religion as *a dream*, range at large in a land of liberty, EXCEPT ONE. Should an individual of any of the remaining sixty-three, or even an unbeliever himself become A CATHOLIC, and send for a clergyman,

man, who in confcience cannot refufe his affiftance, the one is perfecuted for following *the dictates of his confcience*, and the other, for complying with what he deems, *the obligation of charity*; and by implication, both are confidered as unworthy to live here, or enjoy eternal felicity hereafter, let their lives be ever fo moral or virtuous.

THE proteftant religion, Sir, *in your opinion*, boafts its divine origin, the knowledge of the fcriptures, and the fuperior abilities of its minifters when put in competition with thofe of the catholic clergy of this kingdom. It is moreover incumbered with lefs myfteries, and lays lefs reftraints, both on the reafon and fenfes of man, though it does not encourage vice, nor countenance any diforder. It has befides, all temporal advantages—honours—dignities, &c. laid open to its profeffors. In a word, you are convinced that it has God to fupport it on the one hand, and the fplendor of this world on the other. It gained ground, when its foes were more powerful and numerous, than at prefent.

GIVE

Give not the public then, *directly* or *indirectly*, to underſtand, that you diſtruſt *the ſolidity* of its foundations, by fencing it with the BRAZEN WALLS of proſcriptions and perſecution. Let the fabric ſtand, without new tempering the cement that unites its ſtones with the blood or tears of a fellow creature. Hang me, Sir, if I would purchaſe a kingdom at the expence of the life or liberty of a proteſtant or catholic clergyman, guilty of no other crime but that of giving me his ſpiritual aſſiſtance when *I ſolicited his aid* or aſk his advice, or when another does the ſame.

When ſome pretendedly zealous Peers oppoſed the relaxation of the penal laws againſt the catholic clergy of England, on the ground of ſecuring the eſtabliſhed religion againſt the invaſions of popery, the lord Chancellor wiſely remarked, " That nothing was more natural to a
" man, *who believed himſelf in the right*,
" than to wiſh every other perſon to be
" of his own way of thinking; and that
" it is equally *cruel and abſurd* to permit
" a man to live in ſociety, and *deprive*
" *him*, at the ſame time, of *the liberty* of
" profeſſing his religion." The catholic

clergy of this kingdom, do not intend to deceive their proteſtant neighbours, whatever opinion others may have of their religion, 'tis evident they think themſelves in *the right*, as it would be unaccountable madneſs in them indeed, *to ſuffer* for what they deem wrong!

To be plain. When a fellow creature, of any denomination, calls for their aſſiſtance, they are bound in conſcience to adminiſter it; and *their conſcience*, were they doomed to burn in PHALARIS BRAZEN BULL, they are fully determined *never to betray*. They have encountered perſecution under various ſhapes, for almoſt three hundred years; and are ſtill ready to *ſeal* their doctrine with *their blood*. They never go at the head of a mob to break open doors, and *force* their ſacraments upon any, not even upon thoſe of their own communion. They *reject a victim* that is dragged by violence to the altar. They do not go to the houſes of proteſtants to *pervert* them: nor do they erect evangelical ſtages in the ſtreets, or hold nocturnal conventicles, the better to infuſe their *errors* into minds, the more open to deluſion, as the ſenſes are the leſs on their guard.

In

In company they do not damp the gay and innocent converfation with the grating language of controverfy; nor upbraid their neighbours with damnable errors. If afked, in a civil manner, on what grounds they believe fuch and fuch articles; they would be thought furly and unfociable, if they did not return a calm and civil anfwer. Under their oppreffions they confider themfelves as *children of Ifrael*, and of a mother that begets few dwarfs or MUTES, for when queftioned about their religion, they do not chufe to anfwer by SIGNS. Dumb people they confider as favourites of the grand Signior's feraglio, and ftill they afk no queftions about their neighbours religion; they have enough to mind and practife their own. If they are charged in the pulpit or prints, as they often are, with *maintaining doctrines which they deteft*, the dignity of their functions, the honour of their character, and the juftice due to TRUTH, forbid a tame acquiefcence under *the odious imputation*; and in this they only avail themfelves of the *privilege* granted by the fevereft judge, to a criminal arraigned at the bar, *to fpeak in his own defence.* They preach to their own flocks in open day; fhould curiofity prompt others to come and hear them, they do not fhut the doors in their faces, nor treat them with rudenefs and incivility; good manners forbid it! and fhould they keep their doors *fhut*, they might then perhaps incur the fufpicion of hatching A POPISH PLOT.

THESE, Sir, are all the modes of *perverfion* ufed by the catholic clergy of this kingdom. *Indirect* ones they are. If fuch modes of perverfion be *punifhable*, let a law be paffed to pluck out their tongues, and cut off their hands; as theywould not deferve the ufe of thofe organs, whofe operation they would fufpend, when *honour and confcience* call forth their exertion.

OR, if freedom of thought, and liberty to chufe a religion, THE UNALIENABLE RIGHTS OF MAN, be crimes punifhable with confifcations, tranfportation, &c. let the punifhment fall on the *pervert*. Muft an innocent clergyman become an *outlaw*, becaufe, when he preaches to his own flock, another takes *a fancy to his doctrine?* though this likewife is the *indirect* caufe of his perverfion. Muft I hang,

hang, becaufe charity and confcience *compel me* not to refufe my affiftance *when another demands it?* or is the catholic religion *fo peftiferous,* that if I adminifter and another perfon embrace it, I deferve *an odious quarantine* of profcription and banifhment, as if I touched *a carcafs infected with the plague?* If our rulers believe catholics to be compofed of fuch *poifonous ingredients,* they fhould rather put them to the fword, or banifh them in one body, and, at the fame time, out of the kingdom. Some may imagine that I figure *monfters* to myfelf, with a view to the ideal pleafure of encountering them; and that no *real danger* can be apprehended from fuch a claufe. It is quite the reverfe. On the enacting of new laws, or the revival of old ones, the magiftrates are more vigilant, and informers more on the watch. *Examples give the firft fanction to laws, and inftitutions acquire ftability from precedents,* until difference of time, change of circumftances, or the difpofitions of the people, render either ufelefs or odious, THE LAWS, that at firft feemed neceffary. Should this odious claufe *pafs into a law,* our eyes perhaps may be again regaled with the glorious fight of a clergyman in the funeral cart, conducted by armed legions to the place of execution.

The world has set us the long-wished for example to toleration. Let us not therefore revive in Ireland what they are doing away elsewhere. Let the clergy either be taken in one line *under the protection of the laws*, or let them be left, as they have hitherto been, *to the mercy of their neighbours*. If a miserable spot of ground is to be granted to the Irish catholics, let it not be on the dire condition *that it shall be watered with the blood of their clergy*. In a word, Sir! Let not the annals of our gracious sovereign king George the Third be stained with the spots of persecution, whilst the beams of religious toleration are shedding their benign influence, not only on the infant states of America, but through most of the nations of Europe.

CANDOUR.

Errors of the Press.

Page.	Line.	for	read
3	3	controverſey	controverſy
3	14	deliberaton	deliberation
33	16	perſuaoſin	perſuaſion
48	4	*precantibus*	*peccantibus*
68	21	*Paximus*	*Proximus.*
87	21	Sixy-four	Sixty-four

www.ingramcontent.com/pod-product-compliance
Lightning Source LLC
Chambersburg PA
CBHW020900160426
43192CB00007B/1015